Some Songs I wrote.
Adam Carroll

FIRST EDITION

Copyright © 2017 by Adam Carroll
All Rights Reserved
ISBN-13: 978-0-9976436-7-1

Library of Congress Control Number: 2017918436

No part of this book may be performed, recorded, thieved, or otherwise transmitted without the written consent of the author and the permission of the publisher. However, portions of the works may be cited for book reviews—favorable or otherwise—without obtaining consent.

Design and layout: Jen Rickard Blair
Illustrations: Jon Dee Graham

MEZCALITA
PRESS
Norman, Oklahoma

ADAM CARROLL
SOME SONGS I WROTE

Table of Contents

Acknowledgements — vii

Bernadine — 3

Blondie and Dagwood — 7

Highway Prayer — 11

Old Milwaukee's Best — 13

Race Car Joe — 17

Screen Door — 19

Sno–Cone Man — 23

South of Town — 27

Errol's Song — 31

Girl with the Dirty Hair — 35

Oklahoma Gypsy Shuffler — 39

Rain — 43

Red Bandanna Blues — 47

Rice Birds — 51

About the Author — 55

Discography — 57

About the Illustrator — 59

Additional Credits — 59

Acknowledgements

    I promised a songbook to some folks who supported my last album in 2014, and in January of this year one of those guys, Ernie reminded me politely that he was still waiting for his copy. Well, here you go Ernie, better late than never, I'm glad I don't operate a fast food chain, I mean, could you imagine having to wait three whole years for a song burger?
    This book is dedicated to all of the folks whose love, and enthusiasm for these songs makes it possible for me to continue performing them live.

    I would like to thank my songwriting hero, Jon Dee Graham, for lending his talents as an artist to illustrate this book, and for playing "Rice Birds" across much of America, so that I could make new fans. Many thanks to Nathan Brown of Mezcalita Press, and Jen Rickard Blair, for doing an outstanding job putting this book together. Thank you to my great love Christian for being my rock, thoughtful editor, and for encouraging me to make this project happen.

    AC

ADAM CARROLL
SOME SONGS I WROTE

MEZCALITA
PRESS

I HAD THIS IMAGE of a shrimper walking into the Circle K gas station near Water Street in downtown Corpus Christi; This is the one where when you're pumping gas, you're caddy corner to the Corpus Christi Bay. I pictured this guy, with his white boots on, just fresh off the boat, headed in to buy a lotto ticket with his hard earned pay. It's not easy to rhyme "Circle K" in a song, and I couldn't think of what this old shrimper was gonna do once he bought his ticket. So I decided to call Michael O'Connor for some help. We ended up sending the shrimper to a casino in New Orleans, and we found out that St. Bernadine is the patron saint of compulsive gamblers. So when you're shooting dice on a loosing streak, and you need a little luck, pray to St Bernadine. But when you're stuck on a song about Corpus, shrimpers, or down-and-out characters, Michael's the one you wanna call. He's like a hot shot service for dark and beautiful songs alike.

Bernadine

by Adam Carroll and Michael O'Connor

Key of D

Intro: D G D

D   G   D
Well, I hit my stride in Louisiana
D   G   D
Where it's hard to tell the daytime from the night
D   Bm
I placed my bets, and I saw the faces
        D   G   D   A   D
of the winners and the losers in the lights
D   G   D
I dragged my nets off the Widow Maker
D
Up three weeks pay I got a motel key
D   G   Bm
New Orleans sure picked a winner,
D   G   D   A   D
off a run down low rent gulf coast loser like me

CHORUS

             A
Am I the worst you've seen?
     D
Bernadine,
D   G   A
Cast a little of your lovin' down my way
D   D7
Keep these dice from turning cold
G
Make these hard times shine like gold
D   A   D
Shed a little mercy Bernadine

Well the rain fell hard on my motel window,
as the night gave in along the Pontchartrain.
Ran with Little Joe, lost all my money
I got whiskey and salt water runnin' through my veins

St. Bernadine, please don't forsake me
You gonna help me, help me find my way?
If these hard times don't overtake me.
I'm gonna cast my nets into the Galveston Bay

CHORUS: 2X

           A
Am I the worst you've seen?
  D
Bernadine,
D   **G**   **A**
Cast a little of your lovin' down my way
D   **D7**
Keep these dice from turning cold
G
Make these hard times shine like gold
D   **A**   **D**
Shed a little mercy Bernadine

WHAT IS IT that Blondie sees in Dagwood Bumstead? This is a guy who spills hoagies on his shirt, takes naps when he's supposed to be helping out Blondie and the kids, and shows up late for work and is always getting in trouble with his boss. But somehow, she still loves old Dagwood. I guess you might say that for every Dagwood, there is a Blondie out there somewhere. So, if you're fortunate enough to have found yours, please thank your lucky stars.

Blondie & Dagwood

by Adam Carroll

Key of D

Instrumental Intro

He's got papers on his desktop, they're stacked up in a bunch
```
D              Bm         G           A
```
Dagwood worked for decades, he's never been promoted once
```
Bm         D         G    A  D
```
Blondie's got the lunch crowd in a catering cafe
```
    G            D              A
```
She's tired of making meatloaf, it's time to get away

CHORUS:
```
    Bm      G              D        A
```
Hey Blondie you're looking pretty good for a girl who's 82
```
    Bm       G          D            A
```
Hey Blondie out of all those high society women, he chose you
```
    Bm      G                  D          A
```
And Dagwood get off the couch, don't you fall asleep so soon
```
    Am         Bm       G          D
```
You gotta take her up on the roof and take a look at the moon

Dagwood's not the morning guy so he makes the car pool late

The bossman cut vacation back and he never gets a break

The fashion cleaner lady says I hope you're not upset

But your wife picked up the cleaners, she's afraid you would forget

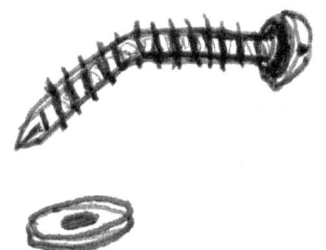

CHORUS

BRIDGE:

  C   G   D
Black and white on workdays, how fast the weekend flies
  C   G   D
Sunday morning colors help to open up our eyes
  C   G   D
She says I love you Dagwood and with that love comes trust
      C   Bm   C   A
I think a little bit of rooftop romance just might do the trick for us

INSTRUMENTAL

CHORUS:

    Bm   G   D   A
Hey Blondie you're looking pretty good for a girl who's 82
    Bm   G   D   A
Hey Blondie out of all those high society women, he chose you
    Bm   G   D   A
And Dagwood get off the couch, don't you fall asleep so soon
    Am   Bm   G   D
You gotta take her up on the roof and take a look at the moon

I've got trouble on my TV, I got bad news in my car
I can always count on those two cause I know right where they are
So I flip on past the real world spill my coffee on the page
And I find that some old couple whose true love won't ever change

CHORUS

HIGHWAY PRAYER MAKES ME THINK of some musician, on their way to a gig somewhere. They are probably missing out on a Thanksgiving or a Christmas, or a birthday with their family, and maybe they just have to settle for a piece of pie at a truck stop instead. They may have been on the road for what seems to them, like a really long time, and even though they may be alone, they are wishing they had a friend to talk to about everything that they've seen when they finally make their way home.

It's a bittersweet feeling that I've come to know a time or two myself.

Highway Prayer

by Adam Carroll

Key of G

G   C   G
For those who the road is all that matters
C   G
For them who have lived on borrowed time
G   C   G
For those who the seeds of life are scattered
C   D
For them that are too far down the line

For those who have lived on next to nothing
Playing in a bar in Jacksonville
With nothing but the songs that they are singing
With nothing but the spaces left to fill

CHORUS
D   G
Here's a highway prayer
G   C
Here's a highway song
C   C
Don't stay too late
C   D
Don't cry too long
D   G   C
You're coming home, home again
C   C D   G
Gonna tell 'em all where you been

I used to think the road was all that mattered
I used to like to live on borrowed time
I used to like to live on next to nothing
But I'm still out here living line to line
Living in some old torch singer's memory
Out here on the road to Tennessee
A place where all our songs and dreams go sailing
I'll say one for you, if you sing one for me

CHORUS

    OLD MILWAUKEE'S BEST IS A BLUEGRASS SONG, with some Carter scratch and some Doc Watson type riffs mixed in, but I think it could work just as well as a polka. If I spoke German, I would sing it at Wurstfest in New Braunfels while I was wearing lederhosen and holding a bratwurst for a microphone. While it is true that Old Milwaukee and Milwaukee's Best are two different beers, I've combined the two as if they were one and the same here, for the sake of the older and the younger generations, for the sake of the folks who drink at home and won't ever make it out to come and see me sing this song, for the sake of unity, and for the sake of America.

Old Milwaukee's Best

by Adam Carroll

Key of A

Capo on 2nd Fret

Instrumental Intro: G C G

G
Lost my first wife to a woman,
G   C   G
Lost my second wife to a man.
G   C   G
Lost my third wife to my cousin,
G   A   D
Lost my fifth wife to my aunt.

G
Said you gotta train them girls like bulldogs, boys,
        C   G
If you wanna keep 'em around.
G   C   G
I got a case of Old Milwaukee,
        D   G
She won't never let me down.

CHORUS:
G   C
I like to drink 'em with my friends around.
       G
I like to suck 'em back till I hit the ground.
     D
They're here with me and
              Em
They'll be here till the end.
G   C
Well the wife and the kids and the dogs are gone,
G
I can't get Jesus on the phone,
G   D   G
But Old Milwaukee's Best is my best friend.

They say Old Milwaukee ain't the best way
For the American boy to go.
I got a dually pickup truck,
I got ten miles of open road.

My windshield's marked with gravel
And my rearview is streaked with tears.
I got the pages of Larry Flint
To show me the honeys of the year.

CHORUS

SOLO

Oil prices are droppin' now,
And my third wife had enough of that.
She ran off to the holy land with Yasser Arafat.
He's got thirteen girls in a harem,
He's got carpets and bags and beads,
But I got a 12-pack of Old Milwaukee
I got one more trick up my sleeve.

CHORUS

Well my daddy was a preacher
In church full of old outlaws.
I've got about as much fear of Satan
As I've got of Santa Claus.
And I've read the Revelations,
I'm not worried in the least.
When you've got three six-packs of Milwaukee's Best
you got the number of the beast.

CHORUS

Old Milwaukee's Best is my best friend.

WHEN I WAS IN COLLEGE, I ran errands for a petroleum engineering firm in Tyler, Texas. Our boss was a brilliant guy, but he was really hard on his employees. There was this one guy who worked there who he left alone. This guy was named Joe, and he kind of reminded me of an East Texas version of The Marlboro Man. He drove a big red dually pickup truck, and when he came into work, you would usually see him wearing cowboy boots and a big belt buckle. He would have his feet propped up on his desk, and when he wasn't on a cigarette break, he was usually in his office reading a magazine and acting laid back and cool. It was my understanding that it was Joe's job to boss around tool pushers on drilling sites, and I'm told that he had a tough job because they are typically the meanest and toughest guys in the oil field. There was a really stunning black and white photo in the office where I worked of downtown Kilgore, Texas during the oil boom there, and it showed a time when the oil derricks literally covered all of downtown. Joe, like this picture, to me, represents that era in Texas history. It may be mostly past now, but it helped to create the myths and the legends that give our state its well deserved, unique, greatness.

Race Car Joe

by Adam Carroll

Key of E

Instrumental Intro: C, F F, G, C C, G G, C C, F F, Am Am,G G, C

```
C             F     F    G C
When the wheels are rolling, he's alive
C     G      C
Going 94 in a '55
C           F         Am
With a burning engine he would go
             G              G   C
Down the Gladewater Highway Race Car Joe
```

Past the Green Frog sign where they sold beer
He takes his orders from an engineer
He tells the tool pushers which way to go
It's one day's work for Race Car Joe

He's got the Camel points from one last drag
Before he takes the grandkids out to Six Flags
The sun has weathered where the wrinkles show
But the years ain't broken Race Car Joe

SOLO

Restless dreams, oil fires, broken drill bits
On a blown out tire, there's all nude strip joints
It's a holy row
He's seem 'em all Race Car Joe

Six foot five, East Texas style, brand new teeth
Now on a crooked smile
In a one-ton pickup, with a cancer glow
When he looks at you Race Car Joe
When he works with you, Race Car Joe
When he smiles at you, Race Car Joe

SCREEN DOOR IS BASED ON a barbecue joint between Kilgore and Tyler, Texas that was called Pat G's. I remember my mom and dad took us there on the weekends to get some pork ribs and some brisket served on white bread. You could see a wide variety of faces there, from a federal judge, to families and church folk, to rough necks getting ribs to take back to the rigs. I open my show every night with this song, and it takes me back to this East Texas shack, where the county was dry, but the BBQ sauce was wet.

Screen Door

by Adam Carroll

Key of G

```
G                             C           G
Lookin' out the screen door through the smoke into your eyes
C                                         G
Lookin' out the screen door through the smoke into your eyes
       D                                  C            G
You're smilin' through the screen door darlin' its worth ten-thousand goodbyes
```

I'm cleanin' up the tables at the bar-b-q tonight
I'm cleanin' up the tables at the bar-b-q tonight
I'm lookin' out the screen door where your face comes in the light

You said you loved the tool pusher cause he bought you a ring
You said you loved the tool pusher cause he bought you a ring
I pledged my love a thousand times while I was hidin' behind the coke bottle machine

I make a wish when you're not watchin' but I keep my fingers crossed
Yeah its only wishful thinkin' but I keep my fingers crossed
While you take the old mans orders on the checkered table cloth

You ask me what have I got darlin when I go back home
You ask me what have I got darlin when I go back home
I got a trash sack full of rib bones and a pocket full of songs

And they're all for you

You're waiting for the tool pusher I'm turnin' out the lights
You're waiting for the tool pusher I'm turnin' out the lights
He's got Kilgore on his collar you know how you can tell he's got
a lipstick stain tonight

I got grease from washin' dishes you got a nametag on your chest
I got grease from washin' dishes you got a nametag on your chest
You're walkin' out the screen door and the smoke is all that's left

SNO–CONE MAN WAS INTENDED to be an epic story about a relationship between a girl working at a concession stand and a rodeo clown. I must have been listening to a ton of Jerry Jeff at the time I was writing this song. It started out kind of somber and serious, and I must have written about thirty verses on a legal pad trying to make it all fit together. Finally, after getting frustrated and eliminating several of those verses, I took a detour, and came up with the version that fit the best.

Sno-Cone Man

by Adam Carroll

Key of D

Capo 2nd Fret
Instrumental Intro:
G Walk up to C, E7, F, D7, C, G C

```
C            E7
Out in the hot sun standing in line
F            D7
Buying sno-cones in summertime
C          G              C
Buying sno-cones from the sno-cone man
```

How many cones in July have you sold
Can't sell 'em at Christmastime, it's too damn cold
Said the sno-cone, said the sno-cone man

Can't get no cone for a nickel or a dime
Can I date your sister, she's mighty fine
Mr. Sno-cone, Mr. Sno-cone man
Your sister Jeanie she bought me two
It was cherry for love, and grape for blue
Mr. Sno-cone, Mr. Sno-cone man

INSTRUMENTAL

He gave me directions to her whereabouts
Said if she likes you, you should ask her out
Thank you Sno-cone, thank you Sno-cone man
She's got a big, big boyfriend, he might give me a whipping

He bought me a yellow one and called me chicken
He said, "you're a chicken"
I said, "thank you Sno-cone, thank Sno-cone man."

Took my yellow sno–cone, I was on my way
Stopped and bought a pretty rose bouquet
With the Sno–cone, with the Sno–cone man
Found her house, she was at the door
Sno–cone cups scattered on the floor

She saw my flowers, she said everybody knows
A yellow sno–cone is better than a red red rose
Be my Sno–cone, won't you be my Sno–cone man
She cried watermelon tears, the prettiest I ever seen
Gave me kisses and my tongue turned green
Lime green flavor from a Sno–cone man

She said my big big boyfriend, I don't like him at all
He's got a hard head and his sno–cone's small
Little Sno–cone, little Sno–cone man

INSTRUMENTAL

She took me upstairs and we sang this song
Been making sno–cones all day long
Me and Jeanie making sno–cone love
I asked Jeanie would you be my wife?
And sell me sno–cones at half the price?
Sell me sno–cones from the Sno-cone man

We got married and we said I do
It was a cone for me, it was a cone for you
Got married by the Sno–cone man
Had a reception at the sno–cone stand
Had our honeymoon in sno–cone land
Compliments of the Sno–cone man

I REMEMBER WONDERING one time what it would have been like if the poet Wordsworth had ever taken any East Texas road trips down Highway 21 with his friends in a burnt orange station wagon that belonged to his mom and dad. I wondered if he would ever have driven to College Station, to go to a football game with his cousin at Texas A&M, where he would then get to drink beer underage, and sheepishly stare at some college girls, and also witness ring dunking at the Dixie Chicken. Finally, I wondered if he would ever have had his station wagon get stuck on a red dirt logging road, while he was trying to sneak into his great Uncle's hunting cabin, where he would then have to get his car pulled out of the mud by a stranger in an eighteen wheeler who smelled like Cool cigarettes and Mad Dog 20/20. I guess I was trying to imagine what Wordsworth would write about if he had been... hypothetically, possibly... oh, let's say... somewhat, if not remotely... a guy kind of... like me. Oh, and he would have also had to have been listening to a whole lot of Ray Wylie Hubbard records, with nothing to show for his ten years of junior college but hopes and dreams instead of a bachelor's degree.

South of Town

by Adam Carroll

Key of E

Capo 2nd Fret

Instrumental Intro: D, G, D, G, D, G, C walk down to G x 2

```
D       G        D        G
```
I went to the barroom last night, I promised not to drink
```
 Bm      G          D        G
```
before I went out the door that night I should have promised not to think
```
   Bm              G          Bm         G
```
About the flipside of my actions when I came home alone
```
  F#m              Bm                G          A
```
but I'm leavin' too so if you come back you can expect to find me gone

CHORUS
```
    Bm                    G
```
And if you wonder where I am tell you where I'll be
```
Bm                       G       Em              G
```
Don't use a map or a directory cuz' I don't like making plans or problems
```
D      C     G      Em               G
```
I just like knockin' around cuz' doing nothing feels like something
```
          C    G    D
```
when your somewhere south of town

Trees bring shade to a porch swing morning, the air smells somewhat clean
My only luxuries are my memories and they make room for my dreams
And pastures I've seen lots of pastures and dirt roads I see one
It may not take me to a destination but my destiny is just begun

REPEAT CHORUS

(I just like making the rounds)

Bm   G   D
Maybe tomorrow you can find another man
Bm   F#m   G   A
tomorrow won't take care of today, tomorrow is the second hand
 Bm   F#m   G   A
And postcards say I'm sorry for lack of a better of a word
  C   G   Em   A
but goodbye says I'll love you, goodbye I never heard

INSTRUMENTAL

You can go to Puerto Rico spend your weekdays in the sun

and you can kill time looking at historical markers along the Highway 21

But if you drive as far Crockett, TX or if you get on a plane

You can think of me in terms of your memories but you'll never hear me complain

CHORUS

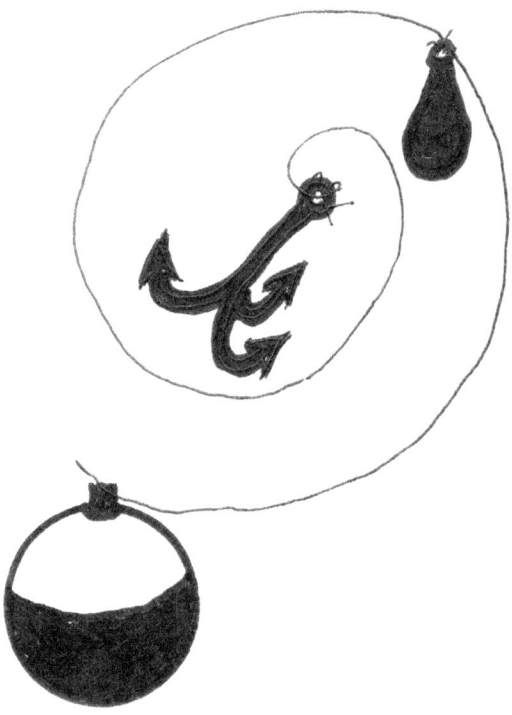

THE GUY WHO THIS SONG IS NAMED FOR, won the Rice Farmer Of The Year Award for South Louisiana, several years in a row. Errol Wayne Lounsberry, was named for Errol Flynn and John Wayne. This song began as a poem that I wrote for an assignment that I had in a creative writing class in college. I've noticed that Cajuns like living hard, nonstop, and full tilt. The first guy says he can do it better than the next guy, and the next guy is often a close family member or a next door neighbor.

    I never get tired of going to South Louisiana, and "Mr. Errol" has shown up in a lot of my songwriting. I'm glad he got to hear his song. It was his favorite and it's mine too.

Errol's Song

by Adam Carroll

Key of E

Capo 2nd Fret

```
       D                     G
Mr. Errol he lives on the banks of Lake Arthur,
         D                                        A
where your windshield gets foggy, where your back roads unwind
         D                        G             Bm
It's a long way from Shreveport, not too far from Gueydan,
           D           A      G
and it's close to the home, that I left behind,
           D          A      G
and it's close to the home that I left behind
```

Mr. Errol's a farmer, he's a father, he's a hunter,
and he talks to the ducks, and the geese in the blind
He works hard for the lives that he hopes to make better,
and he lives by the graveyard of the rusted combine,
he lives by the graveyard of the rusted combine

CHORUS:
```
       G                       D
And he held my hand, when my boots got too heavy
        G          Bm                   A
with the mud from the rice fields comin' to my behind
      D                        G
We set out the decoys in the dark on the levy
       D
and we walked through the graveyard
         A     G
of the rusted combine,
      D
we walked through the graveyard
         A
of the rusted combine
```

There's coffee and biscuits on the stove in the kitchen
There's a crack in the ceiling, there's a screened in front door
When the fog starts to settle on the banks of Lake Arthur
I can still taste the whiskey from the night just before
It's the Crown Royal whiskey, from the night just before

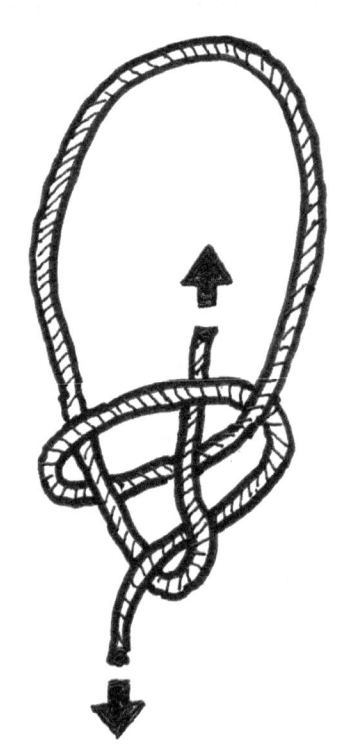

And it's hard to get up and three in the morning;
put your guns, put your shells, put your wine in a sack
We look like some militia, with our boots and our camo
and with a bird dog named Milo, he's asleep in the back

CHORUS

SOLO - INSTRUMENTAL

A combine's a monster, a combine's a savior
lookin' down at the blades, I see heaven and hell
cold steel cut the rice crops for acres and acres
and filled how many barrels? Man I cannot tell
filled how many dryers? Man I cannot tell

From the banks of Lake Arthur, to the Mermentau river
there's water as far as your good eyes can see
At the Lake Arthur Bar; all the old men get rowdy
they got bottles of whiskey, that are older than me

CHORUS

Sometimes I dream of a girl in a pickup,
with her windows rolled down, with her radio on
when you look at the cypress on the highway 190
You give her a wave and you sing Jolie Blonde,
 You give her a wave and you sing Jolie Blonde

Mr Errol's a good friend, he's never a stranger
when I come back, it seems like I've always been here
there's a sign in his kitchen it's written in French
(quand on n'a plus de schlitz, on n'a plus de biere)
"When you run out of Schlitz, you run out of beer"

CHORUS

THE GIRL WITH THE DIRTY HAIR, also began as a poem called "Galveston Bay." I don't know if I even have a copy of that poem anymore, but I remember finishing the song with my friend Brian Rung at Cory Morrow's house in Austin. I probably got the title from a David Foster Wallace short story I read while I was extremely busy not working. I had a part time job my Dad had got for me at a petroleum engineering firm in Tyler, Texas, and I came up with some of my best song ideas while I was hiding from the boss in there. Hayes Carll used to do this song a lot down at the Old Quarter in Galveston, and I thank him for letting me drop his name enough times so that Wrecks Bell would let me play in there.

Girl with the Dirty Hair

words and music by Adam Carroll *and* Brian Rung

Key of F

Capo 5th Fret

```
F           C  G                C
Scar face in the corner, he's stumblin' for a fight
F            C           G
It sure looks good in Galveston tonight
    F                      C
I'm right in the middle of the riff raff
      G                 Am
and the rough necks are wastin' time
      F                G
and the girl with the dirty hair says
       C
she'll be mine
```

Scar face used to tell me "gone are the fishing days"
"the Cajuns fished the red fish all away"
I got that dirty haired woman says she'll be mine until the end
until the Cajuns stop dancing and the redfish come back again

CHORUS
Scar face in the corner, he's looking for a fight
It sure looks good in Galveston tonight
I'm right in the middle of the riff raff
and the rough necks are wasting time
and the girl with the dirty hair says
she'll be mine

INSTRUMENTAL

If I had me some sense, I'd be five years gone
everyone I used to know they just moved on
me and mother ocean stared into the night
all the boats are tied and there's not a soul in sight

I thought to myself 'I'd have done it all by now'
'but I got stuck in Galveston somehow'
she's twistin' and she's churning,
she won't leave me alone,
but the girl with the dirty hair said she'd drive me home

CHORUS:
```
F            C   G              C
Scar face in the corner, he's stumblin' for a fight
F              C         G
It sure looks good in Galveston tonight
    F                    C
I'm right in the middle of the riff raff
     G                Am
and the rough necks are wastin' time
       F              G
and the girl with the dirty hair says
       C
she'll be mine
```

THERE ARE A LOT OF MYTHIC and legendary musicians that come from Oklahoma, and I wanted to pay tribute to all of them, in a way that would go from Bob Wills and Woody and then take us to the present day. But... it was hard to find one character that I could roll all of them up into, so, I finally settled on Leon Russell. He's a pretty good ambassador, and the Okies are a unique brand of outlaws. You can find some of the best songwriters in the country living there right now.

Oklahoma Gypsy Shuffler

by Adam Carroll

Key of A

Capo 7th Fret

```
        A            D        A
He was a Oklahoma Gypsy Shuffler
     D           A         E
Comin' and goin' low and high
           A           D              A
He was a rock and rollin' midnight hustler
         D         A
With his honky tonk wings,
        E        A
And an old snake eye
```

Drivin' down the west coast highway
Songs out the window was all he had to lose
Cutting heads on the chitlin circuit
But he couldn't kick the red dirt
Off his alligator shoes

Oklahoma Gypsy Shuffler
comin' and goin'
He ain't never gonna stay
Rock n rollin' midnight hustlin'
Livin' that low down
Old Red River way

```
         D         A     D             A
And he did it with a bible, he did it with a gun
     A                         D        E
Trying to get away from the damage that he'd done
     D       A        D          A
He did it with a guitar, late into the night
     A                  D              E
Trying to live just like the songs that he would write
```

Snortin' cocaine off a buck knife
3/2 drinkin' in 4/4 time
He tried his best but he could never act right,
With a honky tonk angel hangin' on every single line

He was an Oklahoma gypsy shuffler
With a devil and an angel
Side by side
Rock n rollin' midnight hustlin'
With a suitcase full of dustbowl lullabies

A7
He did it with a friend of mine
D
He did it on the Texas line
B7   **E**
He said he wouldn't have it any other way

Turquoise rings on his index finger
Blowin' them doors off with his blacks and whites
Down the backroads of Muskogee
Slippin' it to some old hayseed's wife

He was an Oklahoma Gypsy shuffler
Always leaving, never gonna stay
He tells the truth, but he's a hustler
D   **A**
Living that low down,
D   **A**
Dust bowl preachin',
D   **A**
3/2 drinkin',
D   **A**
4/4 timin',
D   **A**
Red dirt jivin',
D   **A**
Rockin' and rollin,
D   **A**
Indian gamblin',
D   **A**
Old Hard Travlin',
E   **A**
Red River Way

I'VE SPENT A LOT OF MY LIFE with my head hung down, slouching when I walked, and trying not to have other people notice. I wanted to feel like I was part of the life that I thought others had, but that somehow, I just couldn't quite realize. I got choked up when listened to Scott Nolan and Betty Soo sing this song yesterday, because it reminded me of where I've been, but I hope it also points to a time where I might walk a little straighter, with my head held high as the byproduct of a brighter being, and I hope that others can see this in themselves when they listen to this song.

Rain

by Adam Carroll *and* Gordy Quist

Key of E flat

Capo 3rd Fret
Intro: C, F, C, G, C

```
C            F      G          C
Waiting in the wings, waiting for a sign
C            F                       G
Waitin' in the dark for anything that shines
F           C     Am   G     C      F
Waitin' on the midnight train, waitin' on anything
C       F       G    C
Gotta find something that's movin'
```

INSTRUMENTAL

Walkin' in the street, under neon signs
walkin' with my dreams tucked inside my mind
acting like a block of wood
feelin' that it ain't no good
When the days between us keep on movin'

Waitin' on a friend waiting for a song
lookin' for a bar open all night long
workin' for the cash tonight
trying to keep the time alright
tappin' my feet while I'm grieving

INSTRUMENTAL

Dreaming of a bird, dragging through a storm
feeling like a scarecrow standing in the corn
sometimes you can't get through
sometimes it just takes two
sometimes two adds up to nothing

INSTRUMENTAL

I'm waiting on my wings, waiting for a sign
hoping that the train makes it on time
hoping that it does not rain
I hope I see your face again
with your midnight candle that's burning

INSTRUMENTAL

LOOSELY BASED ON PEOPLE I'VE MET from the area in East Texas, known as "The Big Thicket," who've lived life in the spirit of Willie Nelson—even though they may not have been as famous or as talented as Willie. I was probably trying to write a Butch Hancock song, from an East Texan's point of view.

The characters in this song, like an endangered species, have mostly faded away, but you can still run into some of them in places like Luckenbach, Cheatham Street Warehouse, T-Roy Miller's Pickin' in the Pines, and Bonita Hall in Nacogdoches.

Red Bandanna Blues

by Adam Carroll

Key of E

Capo 2nd Fret

```
D                         A         G
```
Two tie-dyed brain-fried misfits, who lived in a shack
```
                          D
```
in the back of the Bois D'arc woods
```
D            A           G
```
A Caddo guy and a Crockett girl worked hard at stayin' stoned
```
             A
```
as best they could
```
Bm                      G              D
```
Comin' up at night, they were high as a Christmas moon
```
          G                            A
```
Comin' down was the fear in the four walls of their room
```
Bm                         G           Bm
```
They were two hard core junkies, they stayed drunker than a
```
         G
```
bunch of monkies
```
     G            A        Bm
```
They had barrels of laughter with no time left to lose.
```
     G            D             G         D
```
They had nightmares and needles with the Stones and the Beatles,
```
     Em                    G            A
```
They kept all them straight laced business men confused
```
     Em          G           D
```
And the days went by with the Red Bandanna Blues

Ivy was grown over their heavenly home, and their only
companions were the chickens and the doves.
When the law had 'em made, they got laid in the shade,
on their face was the grace from the good lord up above
Makin love in the woods was peaceful most of the time.
But revolution was the last thing on their mind

They talked foul mouthed and lazy. They ate biscuits and gravy,
and they wore blue bell bottomed jeans and platform shoes
They slapped at the insects, and they laughed at the rednecks
They kept all those straight laced businessmen confused
And the days went by with the Red Bandanna Blues.

INSTRUMENTAL Walk Down/ Walk up (Starts on C)

They wore black suspenders, on all day benders, when the dogs were barking (when the world was changing) and the kids were running wild.
They got gray hairs, sat in rocking chairs, and built a great big cradle for a new born flower child.
And they never grew up and they never moved to town
But they kind of faded away when the Bois D'arc's got cut down
They had bad luck and good times, they had cold beer and pork rinds
Sunday funnies were the only worthy news.
They had nightmares and needles with the Stones and the Beatles,
they kept all those straight laced business men confused.
Yeah they were low down and worthless, but they were nice on the surface,
They got by just fine on whatever they could use. And in trouble they got deeper, when they grew their crops of reefer-' cause business and pleasure were two words they got confused. And the days went by with the Red Bandanna Blues.

INSTRUMENTAL Begins in C, ends with a walk down.

I GOT UP EARLY ONE MORNING and drove down Highway 21 from my house in San Marcos to the Texas/Louisiana border, and from there I went to Mr. Errol's house in Lake Arthur, Louisiana. It was a very spur of the moment trip, and I waited until I was halfway there before I let him know that I was even coming. He and his wife Yvonne seemed surprised, but not unhappy to see me, and they made me some étouffée, just like I'd hoped they would. I remember Mr. Errol answered a phone call and said something like "Adam showed up here, cuz he said he wants to write more songs about South Louisiana. 'But he's already got one.'"

Mr. Errol used to shoot at black birds, which he called "Rice Birds", to try and keep them off of his rice fields with an SKS assault rifle. I wonder if he ever hit any? I've had my doubts.

Rice Birds

by Adam Carroll

Key of B flat

Instrumental C x 2

Capo 1st Fret

C   F   C
I was thinkin' of you when the rice birds flew
C   F   C
When the false dawn came with the mornin' dew
     G   C   F
You're a thunderstorm ragin' outside my garage
    C   F   C
You're the white shirt peakin' through my camouflage

Solo in C x 2

Solo in G to F

Solo in C

I was thinkin' of you and I won't forget
The tale of the turtle and Bayou Teche
I can not dance, but I can hang on
to some sweet memory down in Oberlin

I was thinkin' of you at the Mardi Gras
Fords and Chevy's like I never saw
I wish you were here to dance with me
to hear this Cajun symphony

INSTRUMENTAL WALKDOWN
Am   F   C   G

Am   F   C   F   C

I was thinkin' of you at the L.A Bar
where I got so drunk I couldn't drive my car
I was dreamin' about you with my 10 oz. beer
dreamin' sweet daydreams wishin' you were here

I was thinkin' of you with the braids in your hair
Down in Houston but it coulda been anywhere
I was dreamin' about you and my changin' ways
I still think about you in my travelin' days

(Lazy C chord stroke)

Well, I was thinkin' of you where the sunset glows
down the Mississippi River where the Gulf wind blows
I was dreamin' about you and the Fleur De Lis
I was wishin' you were next to me

About the Author

Adam Carroll's musical biography is as winding as the stories in his songs, full of far-away places and close-to-home meditations that encompass a career built on countless shows in Texas clubs, thousands of miles on the road with his partner in life and music, Chris Carroll, accolades of all kinds, and still the burning desire to simply... write the next song.

Carroll's body of work is expansive with eight independently produced albums to his name. From studio records produced by Grammy Award winner Lloyd Maines (*South of Town*, *Lookin' Out the Screen Door*, *Live at Cheatham Street*, *Far Away Blues*) through to his latest releases (*Old Town Rock N Roll*, *Hard Times with Michael O'Connor*, and 2014's *Let It Choose You*), Carroll's song credits also include co-writes and covers by Slaid Cleaves ("Race Car Joe", "Hard to Believe"), Hayes Carll ("Take Me Away", featured in the film *Country Strong*) and Band of Heathens ("Medicine Man", "Maple Tears").

For more, visit **adamcarroll.com**.

Discography

South Of Town (1998)

Lookin' Out the Screen Door (2000)

Adam Carroll Live (2002)

Old Town Rock n Roll (2009)

Live at Flipnotics (2010)

Hard Times (2010)

Let it Choose You (2014)

Above titles released by Gypsy Shuffler Music, adamcarroll.com

Far Away Blues (2005)

Released by Blue Corn Music, bluecornmusic.com

Highway Prayer (A Tribute to Adam Carroll) (2016)

Released by Eight 30 records, eight30records.com

About the Illustrator

Jon Dee Graham is a guitarist and songwriter from Austin, Texas, and he provided all of the illustrations for the book. A former member of the True Believers with Alejandro Escovedo, Graham is the only musician ever to be inducted into the Austin Music Hall of Fame three times.

Jon Dee Graham is most well known for his solo work, including the critically acclaimed records *Escape from Monster Island*, *Hooray For The Moon*, and *Full*. He is also well known for his tenure in The Skunks, Austin's very first punk band, and roots-rock pioneers The True Believers with Alejandro Escovedo. Jon Dee has also played guitar with acts such as John Doe (X, The Knitters), Exene Cervenka (X), Michelle Shocked, Alejandro Escovedo, Kelly Willis, and The Gourds and has had his songs covered by many artists, including Patty Smythe, Patty Griffin and James McMurtry.

For more, visit **jondeegraham.com** or check out Jon Dee's bear art and illustrations at **jondeecobears.tumblr.com**.

Additional Credits

For more on book designer, graphic and web designer Jen Rickard Blair, visit **jenblairdesign.com**.

For more on Mezcalita Press publisher, poet and musician Nathan Brown, visit **brownlines.com** and **mezpress.com**.

MEZCALITA
PRESS

An independent publishing company dedicated to bringing the printed poetry, fiction, and non-fiction of musicians who want to add to the power and reach of their important voices.

www.ingramcontent.com/pod-product-compliance
Lightning Source LLC
Chambersburg PA
CBHW080554170426
43195CB00016B/2785